5-Minute Bible Studies

Written by Steven Borst, Joel Brondos, Thomas Doyle, Larry Reinhardt, Joshua Rosenthal, and Roger Sonnenberg

CPH

SAINT LOUIS

Edited by Thomas J. Doyle

1 2 3 4 5 6 7 8 9 10   06 05 04 03 02 01 99 98 97 96

Contents

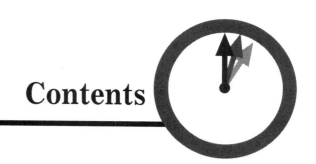

"Gotta Minute?"

If you are like most people in this fast-paced world, your answer to this question is an out-of-breath, "No! I'm kind of in a hurry," "Well…", or "I've got one minute!" Unfortunately, our busy schedules have often hampered or even eliminated communication between husband and wife, parent and child, among coworkers, friends, and possibly most alarming, between people and God. Weakened or destroyed relationships result. For communication is the cornerstone of healthy and growing relationships.

Because of time limitations and other commitments, many adults fail to receive the faith-strengthening power God promises to provide when His Word is studied—"so is My Word that goes out from My mouth: It will not return to Me empty, but will accomplish what I desire and achieve the purpose for which I sent it" **(Isaiah 55:11).** In discussing the question, "How can I improve Bible study attendance in my congregation?" many exclaim, "I don't know what to do! I've tried just about everything!" Rather than "throwing in the towel," one concerned layperson recently said, "If they won't come to Bible study, then bring the Bible study to them." But how?

"Gotta minute? How about five minutes?" Use the five-minute Bible studies provided in this book. Simply, make copies of one of the Bible studies and distribute it to those attending a meeting, a program, or some other congregational function. For many of the studies there is no need to provide Bibles, because God's Word is printed in most of the Bible studies. Or insert a copy of one of the five-minute Bible studies in your Sunday bulletin. Suggest that worshipers use the five-minute Bible study for home study, private devotions, or family devotions.

Although interest and discussion may turn a five-minute Bible study into a 10- or 15-minute Bible study, the time will be well spent. You will provide participants a time for God to communicate with them through His Word, while also encouraging communication among the participants. The Holy Spirit promises to work through God's Word to strengthen our relationship with Him as we build our relationship with one another.

"GOTTA MINUTE? HOW ABOUT FIVE MINUTES?"

Follow these simple steps to provide a faith-strengthening and relationship-building experience for the people in your congregation.

1. Select one of the 52 five-minute Bible studies.

2. Reproduce a Bible study so that everyone has his or her own copy.

3. Distribute a copy of the Bible study to each participant.

4. If you have a large group, consider dividing it into small groups of three to five participants. This will give everyone an opportunity to share.

5. Read aloud or have a volunteer read aloud the Bible passage.

6. Discuss briefly the questions that follow. *Remember:* All participants should have equal opportunity to share their thoughts and insights.

7. Close the Bible study with prayer using the prayer models or suggestions.

8. Encourage participants to keep their study and use it in their personal or family devotions. Or encourage participants to give the Bible study to a family member, friend, coworker, etc.

Unity

John 17:20, 23

GOD'S WORD

[Jesus prayed] "My prayer is not for them alone. I pray also for those who will believe in Me through their message, that all of them may be one, Father, just as You are in Me and I am in You ... May they be brought to complete unity to let the world know that You sent Me and have loved them even as You have loved Me." (John 17:20, 23)

FOR SHARING

1. Do you sense a lack of unity in your family or congregation? How do personal preferences and private beliefs threaten unity and love in the body of Christ? How can such preferences and beliefs obscure the message of Christ and the unity He desires? How did the Lord create unity through His Son's death on the cross? How does the unity between God and people affect unity between those who through faith in Jesus now embrace eternal life?

2. Jesus prays for *complete* unity. Can there be such a thing as "partial" unity? What outcome does Jesus expect this unity to have on evangelism and missions? How does this compare with the philosophy that some churches embrace to "agree to disagree" in matters of Christian doctrine and worship practices? See 1 Corinthians 1:10; Ephesians 4:3,13.

3. Human attempts at unity and reconciliation are often achieved by means of compromise. Jesus, however, prays for a unity which is holy and cannot be compromised. Discuss the differences between unionism established by concession as opposed to the *unity* which follows repentance and confession of the faith. See John 14:23–24 and Colossians 3:14–17. How does this unity affect us in our relationship to others? in congregational matters? in seeking opportunities to share the Gospel with others?

PRAYER

Almighty and everlasting God, since You have given us, Your servants, grace to acknowledge the glory of the eternal Trinity by the confession of a true faith and to worship the true Unity in the power of Your divine majesty, keep us also steadfast in this true faith and worship; for You, O Father, Son, and Holy Spirit, live and reign, one God, now and forever. Amen.

Study 1

Authority

Matthew 9:6–8

GOD'S WORD

[Jesus said] "But so that you may know that the Son of Man has authority on earth to forgive sins. ..." Then He said to the paralytic, "Get up, take your mat and go home." And the man got up and went home. When the crowd saw this, they were filled with awe; and they praised God who had given such authority to men. (Matthew 9:6–8)

FOR SHARING

1. Jesus demonstrated His authority to the crowd in His teaching and in the forgiveness of sins. How is the same authority demonstrated to people today?

2. Consider what is awesome and praiseworthy about this authority as it is given in Matthew 28:18–20, John 20:23, and Titus 2:15. What is the relationship between authority and faith? How is saving faith threatened when there is no authority?

3. In the section of his Large Catechism dealing with the Fourth Commandment, Luther states that "Out of the authority of parents all other authority is derived and developed" (Tappert, p. 384). Describe the threats to our homes and our society when the sinful nature rebels against authority.

4. How does Jesus' authority today to forgive sins—including sins of rebellion against authority—and our opportunity to forgive sins committed against us enable others to experience God's awe?

PRAYER

O Lord God Almighty, author of authority and life and faith, grant that rightful authority may be duly recognized, honored, and esteemed among us that godly peace and order may rule as we serve one another in love, through Jesus Christ, Your Son, our Lord, who lives and reigns with You and the Holy Spirit, ever one God, world without end. Amen.

Study 2

Who's Got the Power?

Romans 1:16

GOD'S WORD

I am not ashamed of the gospel, because it is the power of God for the salvation of everyone who believes: first for the Jew, then for the Gentile. (Romans 1:16)

FOR SHARING

1. The world understands power in terms of irresistible force. Something isn't very powerful if it can be rejected. Do Christians understand power in this way—that the Gospel is the irresistible force of God? If Christ and His Gospel can be rejected so easily, what does that do to the Christian's understanding of power? Should a person be ashamed because Gospel power seems weak in the eyes of the world? See 1 Corinthians 1:18 and 2 Corinthians 12:9.

2. Why did Jesus institute means of *grace* instead of means of *power*? 2 Timothy 3:5 talks about those who have a form of godliness but deny its power. How might this passage be related to the use of the means of grace—God's Word and sacraments—through which God delivers the Gospel, the Good News of Jesus' death on the cross for the forgiveness of sins?

3. What power does the Gospel have for the Christian? What evidence of this power do you see in your life? How can sharing this power empower others?

PRAYER

O Almighty Lord God, turn us away from worldly power that corrupts and enliven us by Your dynamic forgiveness and mercy so that we may be enabled and motivated to serve You as we share Your Gospel power with others. Amen.

Study 3

Out of My Mouth

Matthew 12:34–35

GOD'S WORD

[Jesus said,] "You brood of vipers, how can you who are evil say anything good? For out of the overflow of the heart the mouth speaks. The good man brings good things out of the good stored up in him, and the evil man brings evil things out of the evil stored up in him." (Matthew 12:34–35)

FOR SHARING

1. A viper is a venomous serpent. One particular serpent is found throughout the Bible from the first book to the last (Genesis 3:1; Revelation 12:9). What poison came from the mouth of that serpent? What connection might Jesus have been making by calling the Pharisees a "brood of vipers"?

2. Jeremiah 17:9 says, "The heart is deceitful above all things and beyond cure. Who can understand it?" Before something good can come out of our mouths, the Lord has to deal with our sinful nature and evil hearts. What is it that the Lord would store up in our hearts to overflow into our mouths? How is this done?

3. State the connection between what is in a person's heart and what comes out of his or her mouth in the following passages: Romans 10:8–10; Psalm 62:4b; Isaiah 29:13; Jeremiah 9:8; Ezekiel 33:31. What is the connection between your heart and mouth toward God? toward your neighbor?

4. What does the Lord put into our mouths when He through faith in Jesus has created a clean heart within us?

PRAYER

O Lord God, open our mouths, and our lips will declare Your praise. Through Jesus, let our mouths be filled continually with a sacrifice of praise—the fruit of lips that confess His name. Amen.

Study 4

Closed Book

Acts 8:30–31, 35

GOD'S WORD

Then Philip ran up to the chariot and heard the man reading Isaiah the prophet. "Do you understand what you are reading?" Philip asked. "How can I," he said, "unless someone explains it to me?" So he invited Philip to come up and sit with him … Then Philip began with that very passage of Scripture and told him the good news about Jesus. (Acts 8:30–31, 35)

FOR SHARING

1. For some people, even an open Bible is a closed book. Do you know people who have tried to read the Bible but found it difficult to understand? Who will serve as a Philip to such people today? What kind of studies did Philip have that enabled him to do this work? What is necessary today?

2. The Pharisees knew the content of the Scriptures extensively, but for them the Bible was a closed book. Jesus noted in John 5:39, "You diligently study the Scriptures because you think that by them you possess eternal life. These are the Scriptures that testify about Me." In what way did the Pharisees use the Scriptures? How did Jesus intend for Scripture to be used?

3. All of Scripture points to Jesus. Jesus, God's only Son who was sent into the world to fulfill the promises of a Messiah, Savior, is referred to throughout all of Scripture. What is the danger of viewing Scripture as simply a piece of literature or as a guide for moral living? How does Jesus transform a closed book into an open book?

4. In Isaiah 55:11 God tells us "so is My Word that goes out from My mouth: It will not return to Me empty, but will accomplish what I desire and achieve the purpose for which I sent it." What purpose does God intend to accomplish through His Word? How can this promise enliven you as you share that which God has opened to you—heaven—to those for whom God's Word and its message remain a closed book?

PRAYER

Pray together using the acronym "ACTS" as a prompt.
A - Adore God for His gracious work through the person and work of Jesus.
C - Confess your sins to Him—including your reluctance to share His Word with others.
T - Give thanks to God for His forgiveness through faith in Jesus.
S - Pray that God through His Word would transform the hearts of those who do not believe so that they too may have heaven open to them.

Study 5

Stumbling Blocks

1 Corinthians 1:20–25

GOD'S WORD

Where is the wise man? Where is the scholar? Where is the philosopher of this age? Has not God made foolish the wisdom of the world? For since in the wisdom of God the world through its wisdom did not know Him, God was pleased through the foolishness of what was preached to save those who believe. Jews demand miraculous signs and Greeks look for wisdom, but we preach Christ crucified: a stumbling block to Jews and foolishness to Gentiles, but to those whom God has called, both Jews and Greeks, Christ the power of God and the wisdom of God. For the foolishness of God is wiser than man's wisdom, and the weakness of God is stronger than man's strength. (1 Corinthians 1:20–25)

FOR SHARING

1. "Stumbling block" in verse 23 is the English translation of the Greek word *skandalon*. Our word "scandal" comes from that term. Why was the preaching of Christ crucified a "scandal" or "stumbling block" to the Jews? See Galatians 3:13 for further insight.

2. The Greeks of Paul's day put a heavy emphasis on wisdom. They wanted to figure things out. To them the Gospel of salvation through the death and resurrection of Jesus Christ was foolishness.

The radical nature of Christianity—God offering forgiveness to sinners through His Son who became a man and then suffered and died on a cross—can be hard for the human mind to grasp. How is this evident today?

3. "… and how from infancy you have know the holy Scriptures, which are able to make you wise for salvation through faith in Christ Jesus. All Scripture is God-breathed and is useful for teaching, rebuking, correcting and training in righteousness" (2 Timothy 3:15–16). What means does God provide to create and to strengthen saving faith—to remove the stumbling block—so that people can embrace the foolishness of the cross and receive the blessing of forgiveness of sins and eternal life?

PRAYER

Gracious Father in heaven, when we look to the cross upon which Your only-begotten Son died, we see the height of Your love for us. Cause Your Holy Spirit to strengthen us in our Christian faith and resolve so that we may not stumble over things which are temporal but rather hold onto that which is eternal. Send us forth with Your blessing upon the pathways of righteousness for Jesus' sake. Amen.

Study 6

Make Holy

John 17:17

GOD'S WORD

Sanctify them by the truth; Your word is truth. (John 17:17)

FOR SHARING

1. The word "sanctify" means to "make holy." Jesus' prayer to the Father is that His followers would be made holy through the truth of God's Word. How has God made it possible for sinners to be made holy?

2. Leviticus 11:44 reads: "I am the Lord your God; consecrate yourselves and be holy, because I am holy." Our holy God requires that His people also be holy. What is your reaction to this high expectation?

3. 1 Peter 2:9 declares: "But you are a chosen people, a royal priesthood, a holy nation, a people belonging to God, that you may declare the praises of Him who called you out of darkness into His wonderful light … " How is it possible for God to describe sinners in such glowing terms?

4. The salvation that Jesus Christ gained for us by His death on the cross and His glorious resurrection cleanses us from all sin—makes us holy through faith—and thus empowers us for holy living. How does this holiness affect the way we live our lives?

PRAYER

Gracious heavenly Father, we acknowledge that we daily fall short of Your holy expectations for us. We flee for refuge to the blood of Your Son, Jesus Christ, for our full and free forgiveness. Only through such forgiveness can we be declared holy. Continue to empower us as Your holy people and send us forth with Your blessing through Jesus Christ our Lord. Amen.

Study 7

Abundant Life

John 10:10

GOD'S WORD

The thief comes only to steal and kill and destroy; I have come that they may have life, and have it to the full. (John 10:10)

FOR SHARING

1. The American dream is to have "the good life." What does this mean?

2. All material things will one day disappear. So will the hopes and dreams of people who put their trust in "things." How are "isms" such as materialism like the "thief" that Jesus mentioned in John 10:10?

3. In John 10:11 Jesus talks about the Good Shepherd laying down His life for the sheep. This is what Jesus literally did on the cross. God's Word teaches that the wages of sin is death. How does Jesus' death give us life?

4. "Life" is a term used 36 times in the gospel of John. No other New Testament book uses it more than 17 times. John here is talking about "abundant life" or life "overflowing." Look up Psalm 23:5 and Psalm 65:11. God provides us abundant life through faith strengthened by the Holy Spirit working through His Word. What evidence of abundant life do you see in your life? How might seeking new opportunities to be in God's Word provide you a more abundant life? What are some new opportunities you could pursue?

PRAYER

Lord Jesus, the great Good Shepherd of the sheep, thank You for laying down Your life that we might live, and not just live day to day, but live life to its fullest. Send us forth with this new life in such a way that we may be a blessing to all whose lives we touch. This we ask in Your most holy name. Amen.

Study 8

Judgment Day

John 12:47–50

GOD'S WORD

As for the person who hears My words but does not keep them, I do not judge him. For I did not come to judge the world, but to save it. There is a judge for the one who rejects Me and does not accept My words; that very word which I spoke will condemn him at the last day. For I did not speak of My own accord, but the Father who sent Me commanded Me what to say and how to say it. I know that His command leads to eternal life. So whatever I say is just what the Father has told Me to say. (John 12:47–50)

FOR SHARING

1. Karl Marx supposedly said, "Give me twenty-six lead soldiers and I will conquer the world." By this he meant the twenty-six letters of the alphabet on a printing press. Words indeed are powerful. Share some examples from your own experience which demonstrate the power of words—either good or bad.

2. Jesus says in our reading that the Father gave Him the very words He was to say and that they were meant to lead to eternal life. How does that assurance make us more eager to be in the Word?

3. John 1:14 says that "The Word [Jesus] became flesh and made His dwelling among us." Jesus is the Word of God made flesh so that He could live among us and give Himself to death on the cross for our salvation. How is Jesus God's ultimate "Word" in light of Judgment Day?

4. On Judgment Day our Lord will have the last word. That last word need not come as any surprise to us because it will be the word of Jesus. As a child of God what words of Jesus do you look forward to hearing on Judgment Day?

5. Why is there an urgency to share God's Word with unbelievers?

PRAYER

Almighty God, gracious Father, thank You for sending Your only-begotten Son into the flesh so that He might suffer, die, and rise again for our salvation. Help us by the power of Your Holy Spirit to live each day in light of eternity. Cause us always to be ready for the Day of Judgment so that we may look forward to hearing those sweet words, "Come, you who are blessed by My Father; take your inheritance, the kingdom prepared for you since the creation of the world" (Matthew 25:34). Grant this our prayer as You send us forth by Your blessing. These things we ask in the name of our Lord Jesus Christ. Amen.

Study 9

Getting into the Word

Jeremiah 15:16

GOD'S WORD

When Your words came, I ate them; they were my joy and my heart's delight, for I bear Your name, O Lord God Almighty. (Jeremiah 15:16)

FOR SHARING

1. "You are what you eat" is a common expression. Briefly discuss how this is true in a physical sense. Discuss how this is also true in a spiritual sense.

2. The words of Jeremiah came during a time when Jeremiah pleaded with God to punish his persecutors. He had been given a message to deliver and had suffered much pain and anguish and the threat of death because of these words. Yet Jeremiah talks about the words of the Lord as if they were the choicest of foods. Share some words of Scripture that are very special and meaningful to you.

3. Ezekiel 2:8–3:3 contains another interesting account of a prophet "eating" the Word of God. How does eating make something a part of you? How can you "eat" the Word of God?

4. The Psalmist (Psalm 119:103) declares that the words of God are sweeter than honey. An unbeliever may view the Word of God as harsh and judgmental. Why does a Christian not share that view?

5. God's greatest and last Word is His only-begotten Son, Jesus Christ. At the cross Jesus experienced God's wrath toward sin and offered full and free forgiveness for all people. What "word" are we motivated and enabled to share so that others may also taste the goodness of the Lord?

PRAYER

Gracious Father in heaven, cause us by the power of Your Holy Spirit to love Your Word more and more. Help us daily to draw our spiritual power and strength from Your Word which is food for our souls. As we depart from a nourishing meal to be strengthened for our life's work may we also rise from feeding on Your Word to be sent forth by Your blessing. For Jesus' sake. Amen.

Study 10

Who Is God?

Deuteronomy 6:4

GOD'S WORD

FOR SHARING

1. God commands us not to worship other gods. Besides worshiping ourselves, list five "other gods" that you or someone you know might be tempted to worship?

2. Our theme verse points out that there is only *one* God. How does this affect the importance of the items you listed in question 1?

3. God has revealed Himself to us as triune. This means that within the one Godhead, there are three persons. Our theme mentions "Lord" three times, but at the same time affirms God "is one." How does God reveal Himself as triune in the following verses?

"Baptizing them in the name of the Father, Son, and Holy Spirit" (Matthew 28:19).

"Then God said, 'Let us make man in our image' " (Genesis 1:26).

"Jesus was baptized ... the Spirit of God descend[ed]. ... And a voice from heaven said, 'This is My Son' " (Matthew 3:16–17).

4. Isaiah 40:28 says, "The Lord is the everlasting God ... His understanding no one can fathom." How does this verse speak to those who say, "The Trinity doesn't make sense?" How does faith in God's Word make a difference?

5. Why might "How can I get to know Him?" be a better theme than "Who is God?" How does "No one has ever seen God, but God the only Son, ... has made Him known" answer the question? Why is the answer to this question so important? Read John 3:16 and John 11:25–26 for a clue.

PRAYER

Triune God, Oh, be my stay; Oh let me perish never!
Cleanse me from my sins, I pray, and grant me life forever.
Keep me from the evil one; Uphold my faith most holy,
And let me trust You solely With a humble heart and lowly. Amen.
(adapted from the hymn "Triune God, Oh, Be Our Stay")

Study 11

Pillars of the Church: "By Grace Alone"

Matthew 18:23–27

GOD'S WORD

Therefore the Kingdom of heaven is like a king who wanted to settle accounts with his servants. As he began the settlement, a man who owed him ten thousand talents was brought to him. Since he was not able to pay, the master ordered that he and his wife and his children and all that he had be sold to repay the debt. The servant fell on his knees before him. "Be patient with me," he begged, "and I will pay back everything." The servant's master took pity on him, cancelled the debt and let him go. (Matthew 18:23–27)

FOR SHARING

1. The man in Jesus' parable is faced with a hopeless situation; paying back a several million dollar debt. His solution to the problem was just as hopeless, "I will pay back everything." How do the following plans fail to remedy our hopeless situation of incurring a huge debt with God because of our sins?

"God, I'll repay my debt by trying harder."

"God, I'll repay my debt with all the good that I do."

"God, I'll repay my debt with my good intentions."

"I can't repay my debt, but maybe God won't hold me accountable."

2. The servant's master showed him grace and "took pity on him." How does Romans 3:24, "We are justified freely by his grace through redemption that came by Christ Jesus," describe how God has had pity on us?

3. Through Christ's death on the cross, our huge debt has been paid! Share with a partner what this means for and to you.

4. Look back at the statements in the first question. Why is "By Grace Alone" considered one of the pillars of the church?

PRAYER

Precious Savior, my sin and guilt are plaguing me; O grant me true contrition. And by Your death upon the tree Your pardon and remission. Before the Father's throne above, recall Your matchless deed of love, That He may lift my dreadful load, O Son of God! I plead the grace Your death bestowed. Amen. (adapted from the hymn "I Trust, O Christ, in You Alone")

Study 12

Pillars of the Church: "By Faith Alone"

Hebrews 11:1

GOD'S WORD

Now faith is being sure of what we hope for and certain of what we do not see. (Hebrews 11:1)

FOR SHARING

1. Test your knowledge of great Disney wishes. Next to each character, write what they wished for.
   Pinocchio
   Cinderella
   Aladdin
   Pocahontas
   Simba in The Lion King

2. We often make fairy-tale wishes. We hope that we'll be the next Publishers Clearinghouse winner. How does our theme verse differentiate faith from wishful thinking?

3. Do you hope to be saved? Can you be absolutely certain that God will give you the gift of everlasting life? Why or why not?

4. Romans 1:16–17 encourages us with these words: "I am not ashamed of the gospel, because it is the power of God for the salvation of everyone who believes. ... For in the gospel a righteousness from God is revealed, a righteousness that is by faith from first to last." In other words, we are given the gift of eternal life not because of something we have done, but because of what Christ has done for us. How does this make certain your hope for forgiveness and life everlasting?

5. Look back at your answer to the second question. Why is "By Faith Alone" considered one of the pillars of the church?

PRAYER

Heavenly Father, my faith looks trustingly to Christ of Calvary, my Savior true! Lord, hear me while I pray, take all my guilt away, strengthen in every way my love for You. Amen. (adapted from the hymn "My Faith Looks Trustingly")

Study **13**

Pillars of the Church: "By Scripture Alone"

Proverbs 14:12

GOD'S WORD

There is a way that seems right to a man, but in the end it leads to death. (Proverbs 14:12)

FOR SHARING

1. When Lou Gherig died they remembered his amazing feat of playing in 2,161 consecutive baseball games by inscribing on his monument "a record which will never be broken." In 1995, Cal Ripken Jr. surpassed Gherig's record. Think of a time when you were certain of something, only to find out afterward you were wrong.

2. Our theme verse from Proverbs warns us against putting our trust in human wisdom. Evaluate the following phrases derived from human reason:
   "It isn't wrong if everybody is doing it."
   "All religions worship the same god—they just call him by different names."
   "Hell, if it exists, is only reserved for the most wicked people."
   "Man evolved from a monkey."

3. The Bible says that it "never had its origin in the will of man" (2 Peter 1:21), but instead "Scripture is God-breathed and is useful for teaching, rebuking, correcting and training in righteousness" (2 Timothy 3:16–17). How is God's wisdom, revealed in the Bible, different from people's wisdom?

4. John 20:31 says, "These are written that you may believe that Jesus is the Christ, the Son of God, and that by believing you may have life in His name." Contrast this with our theme verse.

5. Look back at your comments in questions 1 and 2. Why is "By Scripture Alone" considered one of the pillars of the church?

PRAYER

Gracious heavenly Father, I know my faith is founded on Jesus Christ my God and Lord; and this my faith confessing, unmoved I stand on Your sure Word. Man's reason cannot fathom Your truth so profound; Who trusts its subtle wisdom relies on shifting ground. Your Word is all sufficient, it makes divinely sure, and trust in its wisdom, my faith shall rest secure. Amen. (adapted from the hymn "I Know My Faith Is Founded")

Study **14**

The Two Great Teachings of Scripture

Galatians 3:6, 8, 17b–18

GOD'S WORD

Consider Abraham: "He believed God, and it was credited to him as righteousness. …" The Scripture foresaw that God would justify the Gentiles by faith, and announced the gospel in advance to Abraham. … The law, introduced 430 years later, does not set aside the covenant previously established by God and thus do away with the promise. For if the inheritance depends on the law, then it no longer depends on a promise; but God in His grace gave it to Abraham through a promise. (Galatians 3:6, 8, 17b–18)

FOR SHARING

1. Luther teaches us, "We must sharply distinguish between the law and the gospel in the Bible." The Law teaches what we are to do and not do, and is nicely summarized in the Ten Commandments. The Gospel, conversely, teaches us what God has done for our salvation. By focusing on the following verbs, describe how John 3:16 summarizes the Gospel, "For God so *loved* the world, that He *gave* His one and only Son, that whoever *believes* in Him, shall not *perish*, but *have* eternal life."

2. Another way of distinguishing the Law from the Gospel is through the letters "SOS." The Law "Shows Our Sin." The Gospel "Shows Our Savior." How are both of these statements true?

3. Our text points out that God waited to give the Ten Commandments 430 years after His Gospel covenant with Abraham. Galatians 3:24 tells us why; "The law was put in charge to lead us to Christ that we might be justified by faith." How does the Law lead you to Christ?

4. A famous theologian once said, "If Christ came into the world to bring us new laws, we might say he could just as well have stayed in heaven" (C. F. W. Walther, *Law and Gospel*). What did he mean by this statement?

PRAYER

To You omniscient Lord of all, with grief and shame I humbly call; I see my sins against You, Lord, the sins of thought, of deed and word. They press me sore; to You I flee: O God, be merciful to me! O Jesus, let Your precious blood be to my soul a cleansing flood. Turn not, O Lord, Your guest away, but grant that justified I may go to my house, at peace to be: O God, be merciful to me! Amen. (adapted from "To You, Omniscient Lord of All")

Study **15**

© 1996 CPH   Scripture references:NIV®.

I'm a Missionary

Matthew 28:19–20

GOD'S WORD

Therefore go and make disciples of all nations, baptizing them in the name of the Father and of the Son and of the Holy Spirit, and teaching them to obey everything I have commanded you. And surely I am with you always, to the very end of the age. (Matthew 28:19–20)

FOR SHARING

1. List all the words and phrases that come to mind when you see or hear the word "missionary."

2. Compare your list to the list of other people. What does your list have in common with others? How does your list differ?

3. Circle those words and/or phrases that would indicate you are a missionary. What is the percent of words and/or phrases you circled to words you left uncircled? (Divide the number of words you circled by the total number of words/phrases you listed.)

Chances are that the percent of words you circled are much less than the uncircled words/phrases.

4. Jesus' imperative in the Great Commission is for all of us who possess saving faith. Jesus provides no disclaimer for those who feel too inadequate, too busy, too afraid, too . … Satan would have us believe that missionary work is someone else's job—someone better trained, someone better equipped, someone who is less fearful. Why would Satan have us believe that missionary work is someone else's job?

5. Jesus' command is clear and so is His love for us. Jesus went to the cross to suffer and die because of our sinful inability to do that which He commands. He took all of our sins to the cross, including our sinful disregard for His Great Commission. His sacrificial love for us motivates and empowers us to do that which He desires. What will be our message to those to whom we become missionaries?

6. Brainstorm ways that you who have been purchased by Jesus' blood shed on the cross can be missionaries for Jesus in your community, country, the world.

PRAYER

Give thanks to God for the gift of faith in Jesus through which God provides us forgiveness of sins and eternal life. Ask God to provide you opportunities to share His love with others.

Study 16

In the World, Not of the World

John 15:19; 17:14–16

GOD'S WORD

If you belonged to the world, it would love you as its own. As it is, you do not belong to the world, but I have chosen you out of the world. That is why the world hates you. … I have given them Your Word and the world has hated them, for they are not of the world any more than I am of the world. My prayer is not that You take them out of the world but that you protect them from the evil one. They are not of the world, even as I am not of it. (John 15:19; 17:14–16)

FOR SHARING

1. *In* and *of* are two very powerful words. How are you *in* this world? How are you not *of* this world?

2. The *world* describes all that is hostile to God and God's people. This hostility toward God is brought about by sin and is transmitted from one generation to another. How would we on our own remain forever *in* this world and *of* this world?

3. Jesus Christ suffered and died on the cross to purchase us back from this bondage of the world—sin—to recreate us as His own children. Considering this fact, describe your relationship to God using the prepositions *in* and *of*. Describe your relationship to this world using the prepositions *in* and *of*.

4. At times Christians act as if they are *in* and *of* this world. Satan, the world, and our old sinful self lure us away from God. How do we at times try to justify our sin?

5. Read 1 John 1:8–9. "If we claim to be without sin, we deceive ourselves and the truth is not in us. If we confess our sins, He is faithful and just and will forgive us our sins and purify us from all unrighteousness." What do these words tell us about our attempts to justify our sin? God's desire for us?

6. Through faith strengthened by God's Word the Holy Spirit works to empower us to live lives that are *in* this world, but not *of* this world. What does this mean for us at home? at work? at church? in our dealings with our neighbors?

PRAYER

Confess your sins to God. Rejoice in the forgiveness God earned for you through His Son's death on the cross. Ask that the Holy Spirit might strengthen your faith as you study God's Word so that you might be empowered to live *in* this world, but not *of* this world.

Study 17

Beautiful Feet

Romans 10:15

GOD'S WORD

How beautiful are the feet of those who bring good news! (Romans 10:15)

FOR SHARING

1. How beautiful are your feet? On a scale of 1, ugly, to 10, beautiful, how would you rank your feet? Why?

2. Chances are you never expected to answer that question in a Bible study. But the Bible verse for today's consideration exclaims, "How beautiful are the feet ..." Instead of focusing on feet, what is the emphasis of this passage?

3. Considering the emphasis is on the person who proclaims God's good news of salvation through faith in Christ Jesus, once again answer the question, "How beautiful are your feet?" On a scale of 1, never share my faith in Jesus, to 10, seize every opportunity to share my faith in Jesus, how would you rank your feet? Why?

4. If honest most of us would admit that often our feet are not very beautiful—we fail to share our faith in Jesus. Why? Circle the words from the list that explain the reason you often fail to share Jesus' love—fear of rejection; fear of failure; might not say the right words; may ostracize someone; don't want to be pushy; may not have the answer to a person's question. Others?

5. Sin and Satan would have us believe that we are inadequate to share God's love. For our sinful failures to share Jesus' love, Jesus offers complete forgiveness. His death on the cross was sufficient to cover all sins. How does Jesus' forgiveness motivate us to tell others of His great love for us?

6. Practice now telling a partner of Jesus' love and forgiveness for you through His death on the cross. What does His love and forgiveness mean to you and your life? In response your partner can read the passage, "How beautiful are the feet of those who bring good news!"

PRAYER

Confess your sinful failures. Thank God for the complete forgiveness He gives you through faith in Jesus. Ask God to provide you new opportunities to demonstrate your beautiful feet by sharing Jesus' love with someone.

Study 18

I Have Become All Things

1 Corinthians 9:22b

GOD'S WORD

I have become all things to all men so that by all possible means I might save some. (1 Corinthians 9:22b)

FOR SHARING

1. "Be yourself." St. Paul's words seem to conflict with this popular slogan. Can you think of some other popular ideas, thoughts, or slogans that conflict with Paul's words?

2. St. Paul isn't saying that you need to lie about who you are and what you believe in order to win some people for Christ. Instead, St. Paul is saying that at times you may have to adapt the things you say or do so that you do not offend or put a barrier between yourself and an unbeliever. What things might you do or say that might hamper your ability to share the Gospel with others?

3. How might the following attitudes create a barrier to sharing the Gospel?
"We've always done it this way before."
"The VBS program is pulling in many unchurched children who do not know how to behave in church."
"Those people are different from us."

4. *Note:* St. Paul never changes his theology. He continued to proclaim, "For it is by grace you have been saved." Jesus' sacrificial love for Paul motivated him to overcome potential barriers to sharing Jesus Christ crucified and risen with others who may have been different from him—ethnically, racially, culturally. Paul fought the desire to make people like him first before he would share the Gospel. Jesus' unconditional love for St. Paul enabled him to share Jesus' love without condition.

5. As those whom Jesus has purchased with His precious blood shed on the cross, how might you, individually and as a congregation, reach out to people in your community as God's people who "have become all things to all men?"

PRAYER

Give thanks to God for His gift of faith in Christ Jesus. Ask that the Holy Spirit would empower you to "become all things to all men so that by all possible means" you might share Jesus' love with them.

Study **19**

© 1996 CPH   Scripture references:NIV®.

Tell All the World

Acts 20:22–24

GOD'S WORD

And now, compelled by the Spirit, I am going to Jerusalem, not knowing what will happen to me there. I only know that in every city the Holy Spirit warns me that prison and hardships are facing me. However, I consider my life worth nothing to me, if only I may finish the race and complete the task the Lord Jesus has given me—the task of testifying to the gospel of God's grace. (Acts 20:22–24)

FOR SHARING

1. Describe a situation when you or someone you know has said, "I just can't stop."

2. How does the statement "I just can't stop" describe Paul's words in our Bible passage? How does his situation differ from the majority of people who might say, "I just can't stop!"?

3. How often might you eagerly say, "I just can't stop telling all the world about Jesus?"

4. If honest most Christians would probably admit that often their eagerness and willingness to tell all the world about Jesus might be characterized by the statement, "I just can't *start*" or "I just can't stop *not* telling the world about Jesus." Even in these moments God in Christ invites us through His Word to come to Him, to repent of our sinful attitudes, and receive the forgiveness Jesus won for us on the cross. How might you describe this love for you to someone who doesn't know Jesus?

5. Through the Gospel—the good news of Jesus' love for us—revealed in Scripture the Holy Spirit works to create and to strengthen saving faith. How might spending more time in God's Word—personal Bible study, group Bible study, worship, etc.—enable you to respond to God's love by echoing the attitude of Paul, "If only I may finish the race and complete the task the Lord Jesus has given me—the task of testifying to the gospel of God's grace"?

PRAYER

Praise God for sending Jesus into this world to live, to die, and to rise again for you. Confess your sinful lack of interest, eagerness, or willingness to tell all the world of Jesus' love. Thank God for the forgiveness He provides you by His grace through faith in Christ Jesus. Ask God to enliven you by the power of the Holy Spirit to tell all the world of God's love for you in Christ Jesus.

Study 20

© 1996 CPH   Scripture references:NIV®.

You Will Be My Witnesses!

Acts 1:8

GOD'S WORD

You will receive power when the Holy Spirit comes on you; and you will be My witnesses in Jerusalem, and in all Judea and Samaria, and to the ends of the earth. (Acts 1:8)

FOR SHARING

1. Most products and services today come with a disclaimer. A popular car wash posts a sign that says, "Not responsible for damage to your vehicle." The label of a miracle cleaner says, "May discolor some fabrics." A doctor makes a new patient sign a document releasing him or her from litigation if a procedure proves harmful. What other disclaimers have you encountered?

2. All too often Christians act as if Jesus added a disclaimer to His command, "You will be my witnesses." What disclaimers do the following popular responses add to Jesus' words?
   "I might say the wrong thing."
   "Others might reject me."
   "I'm very busy."
   "Let someone else share their faith."
   "It's not my job."
   "I don't have adequate training."

3. To each of these responses Jesus replies, "You will be My witnesses." Jesus' love and forgiveness won for us on the cross even covers our disobedience to His command, "You will be My witnesses." His love for us removes the disclaimers we might be inclined to add to His words. Through faith strengthened as the Holy Spirit works through Word and Sacrament, we are motivated and equipped to fulfill His command, "You will be My witnesses." How might you who have seen, heard, and experienced Jesus' love better fulfill Jesus' desire, "You will be My witnesses" at work? at home? in the community? in the world?

PRAYER

Pray that as the Holy Spirit works through God's Word, you might be strengthened, equipped, and enlivened to be His witness.

Study **21**

Jesus Christ Is Lord

Philippians 2:10–11

GOD'S WORD

That at the name of Jesus every knee should bow, in heaven and on earth and under the earth, and every tongue confess that Jesus Christ is Lord, to the glory of God the Father. (Philippians 2:10–11)

FOR SHARING

1. How might all of Christian doctrine be summarized in the words "Jesus Christ is Lord"? Unfortunately, throughout history people in their desire to make sense out of what seems to be foolish have created in their minds tainted with sin, thoughts and statements about the person and work of Jesus that are contrary to what Scripture teaches. We call these false teachings "heresy." What false ideas and beliefs about Jesus have you heard?

2. In confessing "Jesus Christ is Lord," we are literally saying "Jesus, a man, the promised Messiah, is God." How are confessing these words a bold proclamation of the Gospel?

3. How are the words of the Second Article of the Apostles' Creed a simple but meaningful explanation of Paul's confession, "Jesus Christ is Lord"?

4. God in His love for us provided a completely trustworthy source of information concerning the person and work of Jesus. In His Word, Scripture, God provides all we need to know in order to receive His free gift of forgiveness of sins and eternal life through faith in Christ Jesus. In fact, God left nothing to chance—the Holy Spirit working through God's Word creates and strengthens saving faith in Jesus Christ. How does God's love for us in Jesus enable and motivate us to confess "Jesus Christ is Lord"?

5. How might the simple confession "Jesus Christ is Lord" and its understanding provide you additional and new opportunities to tell others of the joy, peace, and hope God has provided you in Jesus?

PRAYER

Speak together the words of the Apostles' Creed.

Study 22

You Are the Light

Matthew 5:14

GOD'S WORD

You are the light of the world. (Matthew 5:14)

FOR SHARING

1. Darkness and light are two metaphors Jesus used to describe people before and after they received salvation by God's grace through faith. How would you describe those people living in darkness, without faith? How would you describe those living in the light?

2. Some critics of Christianity sometimes proclaim as they compare Christians to unbelievers, "The light is indistinguishable from the darkness." Do you agree or disagree? Why?

3. If honest we must admit that although we confess Jesus Christ is Lord, we are still tempted to sin and at times do sin. But thanks be to God! For we who sin know that when we turn from sin to Jesus in faith we receive full and complete forgiveness. How are those living in darkness different from those living in the light?

4. God's love for us in Jesus motivates us to do what God desires—"Love the Lord your God" and "Love your neighbor as yourself." Through faith strengthened by the Holy Spirit working through the Gospel, we are equipped to live as the light of the world. What does this mean in our relationship with our spouse? our children? our neighbors? at church? at work? Give specific examples of how you might better reflect the light of God's love in Jesus.

PRAYER

Lord God, enable me to better pierce the darkness as Your light shines through me. In Jesus' name. Amen.

Study 23

Run the Good Race

1 Corinthians 9:24–25

GOD'S WORD

Do you not know that in a race all the runners run, but only one gets the prize? Run in such a way as to get the prize. Everyone who competes in the games goes into strict training. They do it to get a crown that will not last; but we do it to get a crown that will last forever. (1 Corinthians 9:24–25)

FOR SHARING

1. What do runners do to prepare for a race? Why do runners prepare for a race?

2. What might happen if a runner who had registered for a race knew that he or she had already won?

3. The Christian congregation in Corinth to whom Paul wrote this letter had heard the Gospel and believed confidently that Jesus won for them on the cross forgiveness of sins and eternal life. They had won the race! Satan, the world, and their sinful nature had tempted some to believe that since Jesus had won salvation for them they could sin against each other and God. They demonstrated a ho-hum attitude toward sin. They convinced themselves that they could do whatever they pleased because they had already been forgiven. How did their attitude and behavior cheapen the grace God had showered upon them? What were these Corinthian Christians in danger of losing?

4. What is Paul's reminder or warning to the people? Why and how are Paul's words important for us to hear today?

5. Paul reminds us to keep our eyes focused on the prize—salvation by God's grace through faith in Jesus. How will keeping our eyes focused on the cross enable us to run a good race in life?

PRAYER

Salvation unto us has come
By God's free grace and favor;
Good works cannot avert our doom,
They help and save us never.
Faith looks to Jesus Christ alone,
Who did for all the world atone;
He is our one Redeemer. (from the hymn "Salvation Unto Us Has Come")

Study 24

Who Is My Neighbor?

Luke 10:27–29

GOD'S WORD

He answered: " 'Love the Lord your God with all your heart and with all your soul and with all your strength and with all your mind'; and, 'Love your neighbor as your-self.' " "You have answered correctly," Jesus replied. "Do this and you will live." But he wanted to justify himself, so he asked Jesus, "And who is my neighbor?" (Luke 10:27–29)

FOR SHARING

1. Jesus went on to answer the man by telling a parable. Read Luke 10:30–37. How was the Samaritan a neighbor to the beaten man? What did he do to show mercy to him? What commandment does Jesus give us?

2. Jesus charges us to do the same, showering anyone in need with acts of loving compassion. The priest and the Levite had to take steps to avoid being neighbors to the beaten man. Can you think of any steps that you have taken in order to avoid being a neighbor?

3. Samaritans and Jews were enemies in ancient times. How might the Jewish innkeeper and the people in the Jewish town have received a Samaritan leading a beaten Jew into town?

4. Even though they were enemies, the Samaritan became the man's neighbor by showing mercy. Sin makes us enemies of God. How did Jesus become our neighbor? What was His ultimate act of demonstrating mercy to us? How does His love for us motivate us to demonstrate mercy to others?

PRAYER

Ask God to forgive you for failing to be a neighbor. Rest assured in His mercy. Ask God to grant you His Spirit that you may respond to this gift by becoming a neighbor to someone in need, reflecting the mercy He first showed us through Christ.

Study 25

Take Up Your Cross

Mark 8:34b

GOD'S WORD

If anyone would come after Me, he must deny himself and take up his cross and follow Me. (Mark 8:34b)

FOR SHARING

1. Who or what is most important in your life?

2. Many people in their search for happiness and meaning to life have swallowed many of the ideologies of the New Age movement. They seek enlightenment and fulfillment in self-help literature, in meditating on their own goodness, in trying hard to get in touch with themselves. How do Jesus' words strike hard against "meism"? Instead of finding fulfillment in life by looking inward, what does Jesus tell people to do?

3. Jesus' words are not new. Instead they simply restate the First Commandment, "You shall have no other gods before Me" (Exodus 20:3). How do Jesus' words echo the First Commandment? How does self sometimes become a god in people's lives? your life?

4. The picture Jesus paints in these words is that of a person already condemned and forced to carry the cross to the place of execution. Cross bearing demonstrates a willingness to suffer and die for the Lord's sake—to give up whatever might keep you from following Jesus. What do people risk if they don't cast aside those things that would keep them from following Jesus?

5. Jesus' words foreshadow His action on our behalf—action taken because of our inability to do what God desired. How did Jesus accomplish for us that which on our own we could never do?

6. What does Jesus taking up His cross for us and then in the greatest act of selfless love—losing His life on the cross for us—mean for your life? How might you in response to His love for you deny yourself, take up your cross, and follow Him—at home? at the office? at church?

PRAYER

"Take up your cross," the Savior said,
"If you would My disciple be;
Forsake the past, and come this day,
And humbly follow after me." (from the hymn "Take Up Your Cross")

Study 26

Creating a Healthy Family

Ephesians 6:4

GOD'S WORD

Fathers, do not exasperate your children; instead, bring them up in the training and instruction of the Lord. (Ephesians 6:4)

FOR SHARING

1. Dr. Nick Stinnett surveyed over 3,000 "healthy" families and discovered six common characteristics. They are (a) high level of commitment; (b) time together; (c) faith and trust in God; (d) good communication; (e) appreciation of one another; and (f) ability to handle crises positively.
How can following the instructions of Ephesians 6:4 help a father (and/or mother) develop a healthier family?

2. The first instruction is that fathers should not "exasperate" their children. What words might serve as modern-day synonyms for "exasperate?" In what ways can fathers exasperate their children?

3. The Greek words for "training and instruction" are *paideia*, meaning "education by discipline," and *nouthesia*, meaning "education by word of mouth." Give examples of when both "training" and "instruction" are necessary.

4. Why is the most important truth for a father or a mother to instruct his/her children, "For it is by grace you have been saved, through faith—and this not from yourselves, it is the gift of God" (Ephesians 2:8)? How can these words be meaningful to parents especially when because of sin, they fall short of God's expectations?

PRAYER

Lord God, we come before You
thanking You for those who instructed us "in the Lord";
asking for forgiveness for those times we've "exasperated" our children,
and asking for help to train and to instruct our children in the way they should go.
Through Jesus Christ our Lord. Amen.

Study **27**

© 1996 CPH   Scripture references:NIV®.

Chronic Pain

Isaiah 53:3

GOD'S WORD

He was despised and rejected by men, a man of sorrows, and familiar with suffering. (Isaiah 53:3)

FOR SHARING

1. Chronic pain is defined as pain that lasts over six months. A person who experiences such pain often thinks no one really understands what he/she feels, and, perhaps, they don't. However, Isaiah reminds us that someone does understand. Who is Isaiah speaking of?

2. With pen in hand underline what Jesus experienced to pay for our sins.

3. What comfort do you find in knowing that Jesus was "familiar with suffering"?

4. Suppose a friend of yours speaks to you of his/her chronic pain. What might you say to him/her?

PRAYER

Lord God, we confess that at times we feel as if no one really understands how we're feeling.

Thank You, Jesus, that You do understand for You were "despised and rejected by men, a man of sorrows, and familiar with suffering," in order to pay for our sins.

Pour out Your Holy Spirit upon us, comfort us, and empower us to live more Christlike lives.

In Jesus' name we pray. Amen.

Study 28

Moving On after Divorce

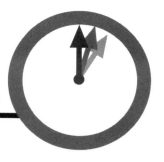

John 4:14

GOD'S WORD

Whoever drinks the water I give him will never thirst. Indeed, the water I give him will become in him a spring of water welling up to eternal life. (John 4:14)

FOR SHARING

1. Jesus met a woman at a place called Jacob's Well. She had been married and divorced five times. Though some would have condemned her, what did Jesus offer her?

2. In the story, the woman tries to change the conversation with Jesus, but He wouldn't let her. Why do you think she wanted to change the conversation? Why do many divorced people feel uncomfortable talking to "religious people" about their divorce?

3. Though the woman didn't want to talk about her personal life, Jesus kept bringing her back to what was most important—her need for forgiveness and a new life. In what way did Jesus provide for our greatest need? How does Jesus' love for you provide you a new beginning?

4. How might Christian congregations better provide an environment of acceptance for all people—especially those who have experienced the trauma of divorce—as they respond to God's acceptance of them through Christ Jesus?

PRAYER

Thank God for the forgiveness He gives to you through Jesus Christ.

Ask God to provide healing to those who are divorced and feel isolated from "religious people."

Ask God to open the hearts of those in the community of faith to be loving toward those who are divorced.

Study 29

© 1996 CPH   Scripture references:NIV®.

Being a Single Parent

Isaiah 58:11–12

God's Word

The Lord will guide you always; He will satisfy your needs in a sun-scorched land and will strengthen your frame. You will be like a well-watered garden, like a spring whose waters never fail. Your people will rebuild the ancient ruins and will raise up the age-old foundations; you will be called Repairer of Broken Walls, Restorer of Streets with Dwellings. (Isaiah 58:11–12)

For Sharing

1. A single parent speaks for many: "I'm so busy making a living and making sure my children's needs are met that I don't have time to care about myself … and to tell you the truth, I'm not so sure anyone else cares about me or my happiness!" Name some special needs of a single parent.

2. In what ways do the verses above speak to the following special concerns voiced by single parents:
   a. "I feel alone. …"
   b. "I feel overwhelmed. …"
   c. "It's hard for me to even make ends meet. I feel like I can't give my children all the things they really need. …"

3. Though some single parents may feel like they live in ruins, what hope can we offer to them according to Isaiah?

4. One of the biggest concerns of most single parents is guilt—guilt they don't have more time to spend with their children, guilt because they can't provide everything they would like for their children, guilt because of a divorce. Jesus Christ lived, died, and rose to repair and to restore those broken by sin. Jesus took not only our sin, but also our guilt caused by sin to the cross. What comfort can every single parent be assured of through the person and work of Jesus?

5. Though some single parents may feel like they live in ruins, what hope can we offer them according to Isaiah?

Prayer

Lord God, grant unto us the assurance as spoken by Isaiah: "[I] will guide you always; [I] will satisfy your needs in a sun-scorched land and will strengthen your frame." Through Jesus Christ the Repairer and Restorer. Amen.

Study 30

Abortion: God's View

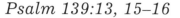

Psalm 139:13, 15–16

GOD'S WORD

For You created my inmost being; You knit me together in my mother's womb … My frame was not hidden from You when I was made in the secret place. When I was woven together in the depths of the earth, Your eyes saw my unformed body. All the days ordained for me were written in Your book before one of them came to be. (Psalm 139:13, 15–16)

FOR SHARING

1. A company in California had rented a storage cubicle. After months of failing to pay rent for the space, the facility repossessed the cubicle and went in to clean it out. What the workers discovered sickened some to the point where they refused to go back. Over 17,000 babies were found floating in formaldehyde-filled containers. They had been aborted, many of them completely formed. The controversy that arose was whether or not the babies should be considered "corpses" or just "pregnancy tissue." Considering the verse above, what do you think God would say?

2. The psalmist reminds us that God is more than the Creator of life, He also is sovereign, making plans for His created. How does this speak to abortion?

3. Consider the fact that 1.5 million babies are legally aborted each year in the United States. What does this say about our nation's regard for God's Word?

4. Sin brings about the destruction of life. Jesus came to earth to suffer and die for all sin, including the sin of abortion. There is no sin too great for God to forgive. How will this fact affect your congregation as it ministers to those who have had abortions? as it strives to preserve the lives of unborn babies?

PRAYER

Pray that the Holy Spirit would work mightily through God's Word of Law and Gospel to transform the hearts and minds of those who support abortion and to cause those who have had an abortion to repent and experience the joy of God's forgiveness in Christ Jesus.

Study 31

Sanctity of Life

Genesis 9:6

GOD'S WORD

Whoever sheds the blood of man, by man shall his blood be shed; for in the image of God has God made man. (Genesis 9:6)

FOR SHARING

1. What is the basis for the "sanctity of life" according to Genesis 9:6?

2. Although the image of God was shattered by sin, God sent His only Son, Jesus, to restore that which was broken. Through His life, death, and resurrection, Jesus recreates us through faith into God's image—a holy people. As those recreated by Jesus into God's image we are motivated to support and preserve life. Franky Schaeffer in his book, *A Time for Anger,* wrote,

"A hue and cry arose after the Second World War because the railroad tracks to Auschwitz were never bombed by the allies, even though they knew that hundreds of thousands of Jews and Slovaks were being transported by them to their deaths. I wonder how future generations (if there are any) will regard those of us with Judeo-Christian principles today if we do not respond to the holocaust in our own time. The insanity of the social engineers and the purveyors of economic final solutions must be stopped" (*A Time for Anger*, Franky Schaeffer, Westchester, IL: Crossway Books, 1982, pp. 160-61).

Identify some specific ways you, as those recreated by Christ into the image of God, might help preserve the "sanctity of life."

3. God desires to save all people by His grace through faith in Christ Jesus. How might preserving and encouraging life give God the opportunity to provide the gift of forgiveness of sins and eternal life to someone?

4. How might God's desire to save all people direct our words and actions as we support and encourage the sanctity of life?

PRAYER

Thank God for the life He has given you.

Ask forgiveness for the times you've been silent when innocent lives are being taken and life itself has been cheapened.

Pray that God would make you courageous in standing up for the "sanctity of life."

Ask that God might use your words and actions to share His love with others so that through Jesus, the life giver, they too might experience His salvation.

Study 32

The New Political Hotbox: Euthanasia

Proverbs 31:8

GOD'S WORD

Speak up for those who cannot speak for themselves, for the rights of all who are destitute. (Proverbs 31:8)

FOR SHARING

1. According to The American Heritage Dictionary of the English Language (Houghton Mifflin Co., Boston, 1971) "euthanasia is the action of inducing the painless death of a person for reasons assumed to be merciful." How does that definition compare to what is stated in Luther's Small Catechism (CPH, St. Louis, Mo., 1991, p. 76)?

"The severely handicapped, infirm, helpless, and aged are persons in the sight of God with life given by Him and to be ended only by Him."

2. Rephrase in your own words the teaching of Proverbs 31:8 as you consider the dictionary definition of euthanasia.

3. St. Paul reminds us: "Do you not know that your body is a temple of the Holy Spirit, who is in you, whom you have received from God? You are not your own; you were bought at a price" (1 Corinthians 6:19). The price for our purchase back from sin was Jesus' death on the cross. How do St. Paul's words speak to those who may consider inducing painless death for a person for reasons assumed to be merciful? A person who has requested euthanasia in a living will?

4. How might we speak up for those who cannot speak up for themselves while still demonstrating through our words and our actions that Jesus bought us back from sin by His blood on the cross?

PRAYER

Lord God, make us courageous enough to "speak up for those who cannot speak for themselves, for the rights of all who are destitute" (Proverbs 31:8). Through Jesus Christ. Amen.

Study 33

Suicide: When There Doesn't Seem to Be Any Other Way Out

Luke 12:22

GOD'S WORD

Jesus said to His disciples: "Therefore I tell you, do not worry about your life, what you will eat; or about your body, what you will wear." (Luke 12:22)

FOR SHARING

1. Life is a gift, including our own life! Only God has the authority as the Creator to end life.

2. Share why you think self-inflicted death is one of the leading causes of death among teenagers and suicide is increasing among retirees.

3. Worry over many things can lead a person to consider suicide. Nevertheless, what does Jesus tell us according to Luke 12:22?

4. What biggest worry or need did Jesus Christ end for us by His death and resurrection?

5. What words might you share with someone contemplating suicide? (Consider: The God who loved you so much that He sent His Son to die for you, will love you enough to take care of other needs.) Jesus not only spoke loving words, He took loving action on our behalf—died on a cross for our sins. What loving actions might we show to them? Christ's love will motivate us to help those contemplating suicide. (Consider: spending time with the person; taking the person to the hospital, etc.)

PRAYER

Lord God, we confess we are told not to worry about our life, but we do. Forgive us. Help us to remember that we are Your sons and daughters through faith in Jesus Christ. Give us wisdom on what to say and do when helping others who are worried, depressed, or even suicidal. Through Jesus Christ. Amen.

Study 34

Hate: A Crippling Disease

Matthew 5:22

GOD'S WORD

But I tell you that anyone who is angry with his brother will be subject to judgment. Again, anyone who says to his brother, 'Raca,' is answerable to the Sanhedrin. But anyone who says, 'You fool!' will be in danger of the fire of hell. (Matthew 5:22)

FOR SHARING

1. There was once a popular song entitled, "I Want a Sunday Kind of Love." Many Christians want a Sunday kind of religion. They want religion on Sunday morning but don't want to be obligated to it the rest of the week. In His Sermon on the Mount, Jesus made it clear that as good as the moral leaders of His day were, they weren't good enough in God's eyes. They weren't perfect. They needed a Savior! Repeatedly, Jesus made it clear that they were lacking in "righteousness." Though these leaders felt they had not disobeyed the Fifth Commandment, "Thou shalt not kill," of what did Jesus remind them in Matthew 5:22?

2. God's protection of human life went beyond the physical. According to Jesus, what else can threaten a person's life?

3. "Raca" means "empty headed." What kinds of names are common today that could damage someone's reputation?

4. Hate cripples not only the one who is hated but also the one who hates. Why and how?

5. Many hated Jesus and without reason (John 15:25). Yet Jesus endured the hatred in order to earn forgiveness for those of us who hate too often. With His forgiveness comes resurrection power—power to forgive those who have wronged us. Is there someone you need to forgive? Pray God's forgiveness in Jesus will empower you to forgive.

PRAYER

Pray the Lord's Prayer aloud, with special attention to the petition, "Forgive us our trespasses as we forgive those who trespass against us."

Study **35**

Treating Others as You Would Like to be Treated

Matthew 19:19

GOD'S WORD

Love your neighbor as yourself. (Matthew 19:19)

FOR SHARING

1. Everyone knows the Golden Rule: Treat others as you would like to be treated. Though it's understandable, why is it so difficult to do?

2. Researchers at the University of Washington discovered that willow trees transmit a warning to other willow trees when caterpillars begin to attack. They send a chemical signal through the wind up to 200 miles away. Willow trees picking up the signal are able to prepare by spewing out phenol in the leaves, a distasteful chemical to the caterpillars. What lesson is there in what the researchers discovered about willow trees that would be helpful in the way we treat one another as human beings?

3. Scripture tells us that "When they hurled their insults at [Jesus], He did not retaliate" (1 Peter 2:23). In doing so, Jesus won forgiveness for us for the many times we have retaliated, for the many times we have not treated others as we ourselves would like to be treated. How does God's great love in Christ motivate and enable us to treat others as we would like them to treat us?

4. Think about someone you have mistreated or has mistreated you. Think about the mistreatment Jesus experienced because of your sin. In what ways can you demonstrate Jesus' love to the person this week?

PRAYER

Lord God, this week,
Help us to be kind toward others, as kind as we would wish them to be toward us.
Help us to think of the feelings of others as much as we hope they think of ours.
Help us to pay as much respect toward others as we want to be respected.
In the name of the crucified and risen Lord, Jesus Christ. Amen.

Study 36

Sexuality: A Gift from God

Genesis 1:26–28, 31a

GOD'S WORD

God said, "Let us make man in our image, in our likeness, and let them rule over the fish of the sea and the birds of the air, over the livestock, over all the earth, and over all the creatures that move along the ground. So God created man in His own image, in the image of God He created him; male and female He created them. God blessed them and said to them, "Be fruitful and increase in number; fill the earth and subdue it. Rule over the fish of the sea and the birds of the air and over every living creature that moves on the ground." ... [And] God saw all He had made, and it was very good. (Genesis 1:26–28, 31a)

FOR SHARING

1. True or False? God created people's sexuality. Why?

2. Our sexuality, our maleness and femaleness, is not something that was added after we sinned. It was part of people's original being! God gifted us with our sexuality. If so, why is it that sexuality is often considered something dirty or shameful?

3. Sin changed people. People's very nature was tainted by sin. Sexuality became misunderstood, misused, and abused. Give some evidence to prove that the gift of sexuality changed with sin.

4. Though sin tarnished the wonderful gift of sexuality, Jesus came to earth to restore people to the image of God. Jesus died on the cross to forgive us for the misuse and abuse of His gifts—including sexuality. God's undeserved love in Christ empowers us to glorify Him through our use of His gift of sexuality. Read aloud St. Paul's assurance: "Therefore, if anyone is in Christ, he is a new creation; the old has gone, the new has come. All this is from God, who reconciled us to Himself through Christ" (2 Corinthians 5:17–18a). What do these words have to say about our attitude toward sexuality and our use of our sexuality?

PRAYER

Lord God, thank You for making us sexual human beings.
Forgive us for the times we have misunderstood and misused the gift of sexuality.
Help us to be responsible and Christlike in all that we do and say in the use of this gift.
Through Jesus Christ. Amen.

Study **37**

"Bless Me—Me Too, My Father!"

Genesis 27:34

GOD'S WORD

When Esau heard his father's words, he burst out with a loud and bitter cry and said to his father, "Bless me—me too, my father!" (Genesis 27:34)

FOR SHARING

1. Through a series of circumstances, Jacob received the blessing of his father instead of Esau. Upon hearing that he missed the anticipated birthright blessing, Esau cries out, "Bless me—me too, my father!" What do you think motivated Esau's cry?

2. In the bestselling book, *The Blessing,* Gary Smalley and John Trent suggest that there are basic elements to the Old and New Testament blessings—(a) meaningful touch; (b) a spoken message; (c) attaching "high value" to the one being blessed; (d) picturing a special future for the one being blessed; and (e) an active commitment to fulfill the blessing. (*The Blessing,* Gary Smalley and John Trent, Ph.D., Pocket Books, Simon & Schuster Inc., 1990, p. 27).

What happens when children are not blessed by their parents?

3. Which of the above elements did you receive from your parents or grandparents when you were a child? What resulted because of it?

4. To bless someone means "to make holy" or "to invoke divine favor upon someone." Though Jewish fathers had only one birthright to give away, our heavenly Father has a special blessing to give to each and every one of us. This blessing comes by way of faith in Jesus Christ. Jesus Christ blessed us abundantly when He redeemed us with His holy precious blood.

How did and does Jesus use the elements of a blessing to bless you?

PRAYER

Lord God, our cry is much like Esau's, "Bless me—me too, my father!" Through Jesus Christ You do bless us. You give us the blessing of forgiveness. You give us the blessing of victory over Satan, the world, and the flesh. You bless us with eternal life. Thank You. In His Name. Amen.

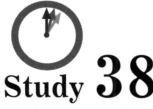

Study 38

What Is Love?

1 Corinthians 13:4–8a

GOD'S WORD

Love is patient, love is kind. It does not envy, it does not boast, it is not proud. It is not rude, it is not self-seeking, it is not easily angered, it keeps no record of wrongs. Love does not delight in evil but rejoices with the truth. It always protects, always trusts, always hopes, always perseveres. Love never fails. (1 Corinthians 13:4–8a)

FOR SHARING

1. A young lady comes to the pastor's office. She is troubled about the relationship she has with her boyfriend. They have been dating for three years, ever since high school. He has asked her to marry him. The relationship has been shaky at times, and she fears she doesn't really love him. She asks the pastor, "How do I know if I really love him enough to marry him?" Using 1 Corinthians 13:4–8a, how would you answer her?

2. Identify the seven characteristics of love according to Paul. Then identify the eight that are not.

3. Give examples of someone who delights in evil.

4. Jesus Christ never delighted in evil, and yet He was willing to endure evil in order to rid us of the consequences of the evil that we too often delight in and do. Because of His death on the cross we have forgiveness and what promise according to 1 Corinthians 13:8a?

5. Examine the love you have for others in light of the words of 1 Corinthians. In which areas do you need special help? Where can you go for such help? Remember, we are able to truly love only through His love.

PRAYER

Lord God, give us a love that is patient, a love that is kind. May our love not envy, not boast, not be proud. May it not be rude, not self-seeking, not easily angered, keeping no record of wrongs. May it not delight in evil but rejoice with the truth. May it always protect, always trust, always hope, always persevere. Finally, may it never fail. In the name of the lover of our souls, Jesus Christ. Amen.

Study **39**

Commitmentphobia!

John 19:30

GOD'S WORD

It is finished. (John 19:30)

FOR SHARING

1. Some say that we live in an age of commitmentphobia. It is a disease where one is unwilling to make a commitment or sacrifice oneself for the sake of values or ideals. What evidence do you see that indicates commitmentphobia is on the rise?

2. When some of Jesus' disciples suggested He would not have to go to the cross, He would not hear of it because He knew it was the only way to earn forgiveness of sins for them and for us; "The Son of Man must be delivered into the hands of sinful men, be crucified and on the third day be raised again" (Luke 24:7). Jesus was committed to finishing the task for which He had come to earth. At His death we are told He shouted, "It is finished." What commitment did Jesus finish for us on the cross?

3. In what ways can parents teach their children to be committed to their values or ideals?

4. Agree or disagree? Commitment is one of life's high risk adventures.

PRAYER

Thank God for His commitment toward you.
Confess your sins of breaking promises.
Rejoice in the special grace God offers through Jesus' life, death, and resurrection.
Ask that God help you keep your commitments.

Study 40

Spending Time Together

Ephesians 5:15–16

GOD'S WORD

Be very careful, then, how you live—not as unwise but as wise, making the most of every opportunity, because the days are evil. (Ephesians 5:15–16)

FOR SHARING

1. In a survey, children were asked what made them happy. The vast majority said, "Doing things together as a family." Though we actually have more leisure time than ever, why is it that families are spending less time together?

2. According to St. Paul, what's the difference between being wise and being unwise?

3. Though we all have the same 24 hours each day, we sometimes fail to use our time wisely and later regret it. Give some examples.

4. Because of the many occasions we fail to use time wisely, God came to earth. What did He do for us according to Galatians 4:4–5? "But when the time had fully come, God sent His Son, born of a woman, born under law, to redeem those under law, that we might receive the full rights of sons."

5. Jesus not only forgives us for our mismanagement of time, but He also restores us, giving us new opportunities to try again. In the days ahead, what specific things can you do that will enable you to do what Paul recommends in Ephesians 5:15–16?

PRAYER

Lord God, help us this week to live, "not as unwise but as wise, making the most of every opportunity, because the days are evil" (Ephesians 5:15–16). Through Jesus Christ, the one who forgives us when we misuse our time. Amen.

Study 41

Communicating God's Way

James 3:7–8

GOD'S WORD

All kinds of animals, birds, reptiles and creatures of the sea are being tamed and have been tamed by man, but no man can tame the tongue. It is a restless evil, full of deadly poison. (James 3:7–8)

FOR SHARING

1. James compares the tongue to the following things:
a. a bit in a horse's mouth;
b. a rudder on a ship;
c. a spark of fire.
In what ways do these analogies describe the power of the tongue?

2. Though people are able to tame members of the animal creation, why are they unable to tame the tongue? In what way is your own communication at times in need of help?

3. If no man can tame the tongue, what hope is there? Does it mean that we must continue to let the tongue be "a restless evil, full of deadly poison"?

4. Jesus did not open His mouth as poisonous things were said about Him (Isaiah 53:7). In not opening His mouth and bearing the sin of all humankind, He earned for us forgiveness for the many times we have communicated poison. This week make this your prayer, "Set a guard over my mouth, O Lord; keep watch over the door of my lips" (Psalm 141:3).

PRAYER

Lord God, today and each day of this week, "Set a guard over my mouth … keep watch over the door of my lips" (Psalm 141:3). Through Jesus Christ. Amen.

Study 42

Pornography

Matthew 5:27–28

GOD'S WORD

You have heard that it was said, "Do not commit adultery." But I tell you that anyone who looks at a woman lustfully has already committed adultery with her in his heart. (Matthew 5:27–28)

FOR SHARING

1. A recent survey shows that there are more pornography outlet stores than McDonald's restaurants. What does this say about our society? In many video stores, rental of X-rated movies makes up a large percentage of business. Who rents these movies and why?

2. According to Jesus, what can be adulterous and why?

3. What does the father who subscribes to *Playboy* magazine say to his young daughter or son?

4. God paid a price for us. The price was the death of His Son, Jesus Christ. St. Paul reminds us, "You were bought with a price. Therefore honor God with your body" (1 Corinthians 6:20). Name some ways we can honor Him with our bodies and minds.

PRAYER

Lord God, You have bought us with a price, the price of Your own Son, Jesus Christ. Thank You. Help us to honor You with our body and mind! In Jesus' name. Amen.

Study 43

"I'm Going to Sue You!"

James 5:16a

GOD'S WORD

Therefore confess your sins to each other and pray for each other. (James 5:16a)

FOR SHARING

1. Some call it "The Blame Game." It's a game many have become quite proficient at. Blame someone else! Make an excuse! A few years ago when a well-known athlete got AIDS he said, "I tried to accommodate as many women as I could…and hence I got AIDS." Why is it that we've become so good at making excuses for wrongdoing? Or are we any different now than Adam and Eve in the Garden of Eden as they blamed everyone but themselves?

2. Contrast the present-day litigious mentality with the words of James 5:16a. In what ways would marriages and families be healthier if they practiced the words of James?

3. Agree or disagree? "The price of greatness is responsibility. Society can only survive as long as citizens are as conscious of their obligations as they are of their rights."

4. Why is it that rights have become more important than responsibility?

5. There is no better picture of someone giving up His rights than Jesus Christ: "Who, being in very nature God, did not consider equality with God something to be grasped, but made Himself nothing, taking the very nature of a servant, being made in human likeness. And being found in appearance as a man, He humbled Himself and became obedient to death—even death on a cross!" (Philippians 2:6–8). For what one reason did Jesus lay aside His rights? How does His love for us make it possible for us to have an attitude more like His?

PRAYER

Spend some time praying silently.
Confess your sins, especially the sin of blaming others or circumstances.
Ask God to help you take responsibility.
Pray for others instead of blaming them.

Study 44

Homosexuality

Romans 1:21, 24–27a

GOD'S WORD

For although they knew God, they neither glorified Him as God nor gave thanks to Him, but their thinking became futile and their foolish hearts were darkened.... Therefore God gave them over in the sinful desires of their hearts to sexual impurity for the degrading of their bodies with one another. They exchanged the truth of God for a lie, and worshipped and served created things rather than the Creator—who is forever praised. Amen. Because of this, God gave them over to shameful lusts. Even their women exchanged natural relations for unnatural ones. In the same way the men also abandoned natural relations with women and were inflamed with lust for one another. (Romans 1:21, 24–27a)

FOR SHARING

1. St. Paul said the people "knew God." Even if they were never taught about God, what evidence is there in the world that God exists?

2. Instead of worshiping the Creator, they "worshipped and served created things." Give examples of the same thing happening in our day and age.

3. When St. Paul says "God gave them over," he means God allowed sin to run its course. With pen in hand underline the cycle of sin according to St. Paul.

4. Scripture is clear—homosexuality is a sin in God's eyes. There is good news for the sinner caught up in homosexuality or any other sin: "For all have sinned and fall short of the glory of God, and are justified freely by His grace through the redemption that came by Christ Jesus" (Romans 3:23–24). In summary, how might you as a Christian respond to a person caught in the sin of homosexuality, or any other sin for that matter? What words of comfort can you share with repentant sinners.

PRAYER

Pray for those who are caught in the bondage of homosexuality.
Ask the Holy Spirit to free them from their sin.
Pray that you might treat homosexuals as people for whom Christ died, so that through your love you might have the opportunity to share God's Word of Law and Gospel.

Study 45

Overcoming Depression

Philippians 4:13

GOD'S WORD

I can do everything through Him who gives me strength. (Philippians 4:13)

FOR SHARING

1. Studies show that people born in the last 25 years are three to four times more likely to be depressed than those born in previous generations. Why do you think this is so?

2. One of the symptoms of depression is seeing things out of perspective. For example, 75 percent of people who are severely depressed never think they will get better. In what way does Philippians 4:13 contradict such thinking?

3. Though God won't make our depression just automatically disappear, what will God do according to St. Paul?

4. Depression is not a part of God's original creation. What connection is there between St. Paul's words in Philippians 4:13 with what he says in 2 Corinthians 5:17, "Therefore, if anyone is in Christ, he is a new creation; the old has gone, the new has come"?

5. How can the fact that Christ who died for our sins, who has recreated us in faith, and who lives in us by God's grace help us deal with depression?

PRAYER

Lord God, sometimes we forget that we "can do all things through [You] who gives us the strength." Forgive us. Restore us. Through Jesus Christ. Amen.

Study 46

The Gift of Work

Genesis 2:8, 15

GOD'S WORD

Now the LORD God had planted a garden in the east, in Eden; and there He put the man He had formed. ... The LORD God took the man and put him in the Garden of Eden to work it and take care of it. (Genesis 2:8, 15)

FOR SHARING

1. Who planted the garden? Who was to cultivate it?

2. Though God is omnipotent and has no need for anyone's help, He chose to provide man and woman the opportunity to participate in His plans. How is work a gift from God in which He gives us the opportunity to serve Him and to give Him thanks?

3. If work is a gift of God, what makes it so hard at times (Romans 8:20)? How does sin affect our work and our relationships with our coworkers?

4. Even though the gift of work was tarnished through sin, there is hope. Through His greatest gift—Jesus Christ—God provided victory for us over sin, death, and the power of Satan. God's love for us in Christ Jesus motivates and empowers us to affirm our work as a gift, enabling us to serve Him and to give Him thanks through our work. How will this fact affect the quality of our work? Our relationship with coworkers?

PRAYER

Lord God, we ...
Thank You for the gift of work;
Ask forgiveness for the times sin has affected our work and our relationship with coworkers, specifically we are reminded of (silently confess sins);
Ask that Your love for us in Christ Jesus might motivate and empower us to serve You and to give You thanks through our work. In Jesus' name we pray. Amen.

Study 47

Workaholism: The Acceptable Addiction

2 Thessalonians 3:10

GOD'S WORD

If a man will not work, he shall not eat. (2 Thessalonians 3:10)

FOR SHARING

1. Even Rabbis were expected to earn their living by some labor other than just teaching the law. St. Paul made a living as a tentmaker. Why do you think St. Paul thought it was necessary to say something about work?

2. Which of the following sayings do you think best summarizes the thought of 2 Thessalonians 3:10? Why?
   a. God gives us the ingredients for our daily bread, but He expects us to do the baking.
   b. No dream comes true until you wake up and go to work.
   c. Happiness is the result of being too busy to be miserable.
   d. The Lord didn't burden us with work. He blessed us with it.

3. Though work is important, when does it become an addiction? When a person's life is controlled by work or when a person believes that the world will collapse if he or she isn't at work, they may suffer from workaholism. What are some other symptoms of workaholism?

4. Many believe, "Work is the one acceptable addiction." What do you think?

5. Anytime, anything, or anyone comes first in our life other than God, we break the First Commandment—we sin. Christ went to the cross to suffer the punishment for all of our sins, including the sin of workaholism. What special comfort do you experience as a result of what Jesus accomplished for you? How can the enormous love of God in Christ help keep God number 1 in your life?

PRAYER

Lord Jesus, thank You for the work You did: "[You Yourself] bore our sins in [Your] body on the tree, so that we might die to sins and live for righteousness; by [Your] wounds [we] have been healed" (1 Peter 2:24). Forgive us for the times we have misused work in our own lives. Empower us to keep You first in our lives. Amen.

Study 48

AIDS: The New Epidemic

1 Corinthians 12:26–27

GOD'S WORD

If one part suffers, every part suffers with it; if one part is honored, every part rejoices with it. Now you are the body of Christ, and each one of you is a part of it. (1 Corinthians 12:26–27)

FOR SHARING

1. One million Americans—one in every 250—are infected with HIV. Within 10 years the majority of those infected with HIV will develop AIDS. This means that most people will within their lifetime know some person—a friend, relative, or acquaintance—who will be HIV or AIDS affected. What does 1 Corinthians 12:26–27 say to each of us as we minister to those with AIDS?

2. AIDS often divides people. How might God use this dreaded disease to bring people closer to Him? To others?

3. "The body of Christ has AIDS." How is this statement correct in a spiritual sense? Despite our spiritual AIDS, Jesus Christ provides us with healing. Read aloud the assurance as stated by St. Paul.

"Consequently, just as the result of one trespass was condemnation for all men, so also the result of one act of righteousness was justification that brings life for all men. For just as through the disobedience of the one man the many were made sinners, so also through the obedience of the one man the many will be made righteous" (Romans 5:18–19).

4. How might Jesus' comfort and healing enable those who have experienced it to deliver His comfort and healing to repentant sinners suffering from AIDS?

PRAYER

Thank God for sending Jesus in order to heal us of sin and death.
Make special intercessions for those you know who have AIDS.
Ask God to provide you with opportunities to share His comfort and healing to those who have AIDS.

Study 49

The Inevitable: Death

Philippians 1:21

GOD'S WORD

For to me, to live is Christ and to die is gain. (Philippians 1:21)

FOR SHARING

1. How might you complete the phrase, "For to me, to live is _____ and to die is _____." Why?

2. Paul was in prison when he wrote this letter to the Philippians. He was not sure of his fate, nevertheless, of what was St. Paul sure?

3. How could St. Paul be so assured that he didn't need to fear life or death (cf., Romans 8:33–34)?

4. Whether alive on this earth or dead on this earth and alive in heaven, for those who possess saving faith through God's grace in Jesus, we live with Christ and Christ lives in us. How does this fact affect your attitude toward death?

5. What can you specifically do for those who are not as confident about death as St. Paul or yourself?

PRAYER

Thank God for the assurance you have of eternal life through Jesus Christ.

Ask God that by the power of the Holy Spirit working through His Word He might touch those who do not have assurance of eternal life.

Ask God to provide you with the words you need to talk to the unsaved about Jesus Christ.

Study **50**

© 1996 CPH   Scripture references:NIV®.

Coping with Infertility

Isaiah 40:31–32

GOD'S WORD

But those who hope in the LORD will renew their strength. They will soar on wings like eagles; they will run and not grow weary, they will walk and not be faint. (Isaiah 40:31–32)

FOR SHARING

1. Isaiah reminds us to "hope in the LORD." This is not just "wishful anticipating." It is trusting in God. How might "trusting in God" be difficult for the childless couple who wants a child?

2. One out of six couples have a problem with infertility. What kind of statements do people make which indicate that many people have little understanding of the problem of infertility (e.g., "Just get away for a week, and you'll end up pregnant.")?

3. Few people know the disappointment and anguish of the couple coping with infertility. Though we may never have children, what does God promise us according to Isaiah? Isaiah reminds us that God "will renew [our] strength." It literally means that He will make an exchange: our weakness for His strength.

4. Amidst hopelessness, God gives us hope. The promise is: "He who did not spare His own Son, but gave Him up for us all—how will He not also, along with Him, graciously give us all things?" (Romans 8:32). In your own words, what assurance does this promise give to the couple experiencing infertility?

PRAYER

Lord God, the promise is ours, "But those who hope in the LORD will renew their strength" (Isaiah 40:31).

Turn our hopelessness into hope. Take our weakness and give us Your strength.

Remind us that we are Yours through the blood of Jesus Christ. In the name of Jesus. Amen.

Study 51

The Partnership of Stepparenting

Galatians 6:2, 10

GOD'S WORD

Carry each other's burdens, and in this way you will fulfill the law of Christ. Therefore, as we have opportunity, let us do good to all people, especially to those who belong to the family of believers. (Galatians 6:2, 10)

FOR SHARING

1. Sixty percent of all children born today will live in a single-parent home before they reach age eighteen. Because of this, many children also will live in what we refer to as a blended family, meaning one or both of the families who join together will have children who are not biologically related. Stepparenting presents many challenges. The word "burdens" denotes a heavy load. What special challenges might a nonbiological parent face in raising stepchildren?

2. How does carrying someone's burdens enable us to share Jesus?

3. What is some "good" that you and your church might be able to do for the step-parents in your church family?

4. Think about it! We were not God's children by nature; nevertheless, what did He do for us? See Romans 5:6–11.

5. How does God's love for us in Christ Jesus—who carried the burden of our sin to the cross—enable us to carry the burdens of families? Especially, families burdened by and with blending?

PRAYER

God, You sent Your only Son to carry the burden of our sin to the cross. Enable us to carry each other's burdens and in so doing share Your love with others. Amen.

Study 52

For more in-depth adult Bible studies...

Find Healing in . . .

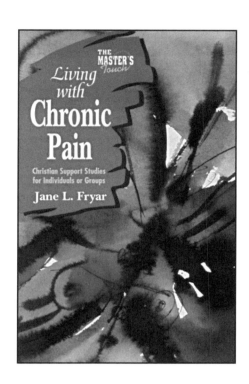

*J*esus' healing touch of love, hope and forgiveness will help you find positive solutions to the concerns weighing on your heart. As you study and share His Word, the Holy Sprit will lead you to grow in spiritual maturity and deeper faith experiences, and even reach out to those who face similar needs and concerns.

Four to five sessions each . . .

Living with **Chronic Pain**
Suffering from **Guilt**
Living with **Change**
Coping with **Compassion Fatigue**
Living with **Compulsive Behaviors**
Discovering **Life after Divorce**
Living with **Infertility**
Surviving **Sexual Abuse**
Living with **Too Little Time**
Coping with **Stress**
Living with **Grief**

Living with **Terminal Illness**
AIDS: A Christian Perspective
Living with **Workaholism**
Surviving **Financial Crisis**
Overcoming **Depression**

Concordia Publishing House
3558 South Jefferson Avenue
Saint Louis, MO 63118-3968

Real lives facing real frustrations need Connections to God and to one another.

The **Connections** Bible study series helps take the concerns of your heart and turn them over to Jesus in worship, prayer, Bible study and discussion.

Connections uses a Gospel-centered message to build trust in God and to develop trusting and supportive relationships with one another, just as Christ intended.

Connections studies look at small portions of Scripture that really hit home, in areas where anxiety is often deepest.

For small groups or individual study, **Connections** uses God's Word to build relationships and bring peace to troubled hearts.

Ask for **Connections** at your Christian bookstore or call CPH, 1 800 325 3040

H54821

Concordia Publishing House
3558 South Jefferson Avenue
Saint Louis, MO 63118-3968

Hear His Voice in . . .

God's Word for Today

GOD'S WORD FOR TODAY

AMOS
And Justice for All

• Inhumanity and hatred • Complacent people
• Meaningless religion • Renewal in the Messiah

T his series helps you hear God speaking to you today — lovingly, emphatically, personally. As you study His Word book by book, you'll find: chapter-by-chapter background information; questions and learning experiences that promote exciting and challenging discussions; and activities that reveal how God speaks to the deepest concerns of your heart.

Each six to thirteen sessions each . . .

Amos: *And Justice for All*
Revelation: *Interpreting the Prophecy*
Psalms: *Conversations with God*
Genesis: *Rooted in Relationship*
Matthew: *His Kingdom Forever*
Galatians: *The Cost of Freedom*
1 Peter: *God's Chosen People*
Colossians/Philemon: *Take a New Look at Christ*
James: *How Faith Works*
Exodus: *By His Mighty Hand*
Proverbs: *God's Gift of Wisdom*
Ezekiel: *I Am the Lord*
Mark: *The Serving Christ*

Hosea: *Critic and Comforter for Today*
Acts: *The Gospel Throughout the World*
Ephesians: *The Church: God's Servant*
Romans: *Alive in Christ*
Ecclesiastes: *Enjoying God's Gifts*
Daniel: *Encouragement for Faith*
The Gospel of John: *Word Became Flesh*
1 Corinthians: *One in Christ*
Philippians: *Rejoice in the Lord*
Hebrews: *Alive Through Faith*
Isaiah: *Here Am I! Send Me*

Concordia Publishing House
3558 South Jefferson Avenue
Saint Louis, MO 63118-3968